little cooks

little cooks

30 delicious recipes to make and enjoy

**Fiona Hamilton-Fairley
The Kids' Cookery School**

For all students at The Kids' Cookery School, past, present and future

First published in 2008 by New Holland Publishers (UK) Ltd
London · Cape Town · Sydney · Auckland

Garfield House, 86–88 Edgware Road, London, W2 2EA, United Kingdom
www.newhollandpublishers.com

80 McKenzie Street, Cape Town 8001, South Africa

Unit 1, 66 Gibbes Street, Chatswood, NSW 2067, Australia

218 Lake Road, Northcote, Auckland, New Zealand

10 9 8 7 6 5 4 3 2 1

ISBN 978 184537 984 1

Editor: Clare Sayer
Design: AG&G Books
Photography: Stuart West
Food Styling: Stella Murphy
Production: Hema Gohil
Editorial Direction: Rosemary Wilkinson

Reproduction by Pica Digital PTE Ltd, Singapore
Printed and bound by Times Offset, Malaysia

ACKNOWLEDGEMENTS
I would particularly like to thank The Kids' Cookery School team for their contributions: John Fernandez,
Alexander Volev, Hilary Byrne and Jo Rudsdale. Thanks also to all KCS volunteers and students.

contents

introduction

Welcome to your new cookery book!

I have written this book for you so that you can learn to make healthy and tasty things to eat and drink for yourself, your family and friends. Here you can learn to make yummy breakfasts, healthy snacks and tasty things for your lunchbox. You can even surprise your friends and family with a delicious recipe from the Family Weekend Meals chapter or try something from Teatime Treats and Party Food next time you have some friends over.

Cooking is fun and doesn't have to be difficult: these recipes are all simple and easy to follow. Use the step-by-step pictures and get an adult to help you. Don't worry if you make mistakes – chefs learn new things everyday in the kitchen. Most importantly, don't be afraid to try new things and experiment by adding different ingredients. Have fun with food and discover your inner chef!

I started cooking as a child at home and have been teaching children just like you how to cook since 1995. At The Kids' Cookery School we've taught tens of thousands of children from three years upwards how to cook healthy, delicious food from fresh ingredients.

It's really important to learn to cook for yourself so you can eat the best food to keep you healthy and active. What you eat and drink really affects how you enjoy life and all your activities – school work, sports, games and hobbies.

Cooking is a skill that you'll use throughout your whole life. Keep practising and you'll always be able to impress people with your fantastic creations!

I hope you enjoy learning how to do new things from this book and tasting all the different flavours.

So, what are you waiting for? Wash your hands, put on your apron and let's get cooking!

Happy, healthy cooking!

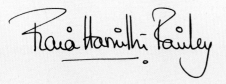

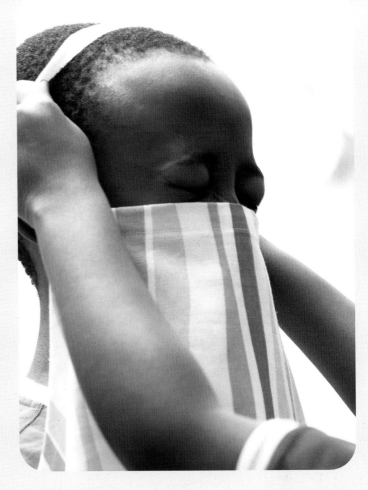

The Kids' Cookery School (KCS) is a Registered Charity which opened its doors in 2000. It is a unique cookery school, welcoming children aged 3–16 years, including those with special needs and those who are economically or socially disadvantaged. At KCS students learn how to cook delicious dishes from fresh ingredients in an inspiring, creative environment. We encourage children to be inquisitive and want to know more about food and where it comes from.

To find out more visit: www.thekidscookeryschool.co.uk

safety in the kitchen

Cooking is such great fun that I'm sure you'll want to get started straightaway! However, the kitchen can be a dangerous place so it is important to follow some simple rules. You will also make fewer mistakes and make yummier food if you are properly prepared.

BEFORE YOU START

- Wash your hands with soap and water and don't forget to dry them.
- Put on a clean apron and if you have long hair, tie it up.
- Assemble all of the ingredients and equipment you need and read through the recipe.
- Make sure you understand what everything is. If there is anything you don't recognise, ask a grown-up to explain it to you.
- Make sure that all the work surfaces are nice and clean.

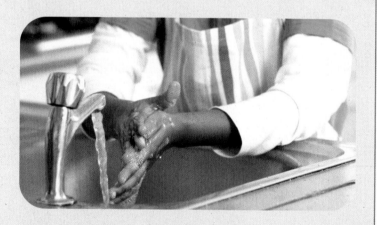

WHILE YOU ARE COOKING

- Remember that sharp knives, graters, scissors and peelers can all be dangerous. Keep your fingers away from the blade and never chop towards yourself.
- Wear oven gloves if you are touching anything hot and using the oven.
- Keep your cooking area clean and clear whilst you cook. Mop up spills as you go along.

AFTER COOKING

- Always allow food to cool slightly before serving. Never serve hot food straight from the oven or grill.
- Everyone should help with the tidying up and clearing up. This part is just as much fun as the cooking!

safe eating Food can sometimes make people ill. This is called 'food poisoning'. However, you can avoid this if you follow some simple rules.

- Always wash your hands before cooking and wear a clean apron.
- Try not to touch your face and hair whilst cooking.
- Always wash any fruit, vegetables or fresh herbs that you will be using. You do not really need to wash any vegetables or fruit that are going to be peeled such as onions and bananas.
- Try and keep raw meat and fish away from other foods. Use a separate chopping board if possible.
- Wash your hands thoroughly after touching raw meat, fish or eggs.
- Make sure you know when meat is properly cooked: get a grown-up to help you check the largest piece of meat. Chicken and fish go white when cooked.

kitchen equipment

There are some pieces of equipment which appear in nearly every recipe in this book so why not have a quick look around the kitchen and make sure you know what everything is? If there is something you are not familiar with, ask an adult to tell you more about it.

You will come across all sorts of different pieces of equipment and kitchen utensils when using the recipes in this book. Here are some of the essentials, as well as some things you may not be familiar with:

Baking beans These are beans that help to weigh down pastry in its tin when baking without a filling.

Chopping boards These are often wooden but plastic boards are much more hygienic. They often come in sets so that you use a different colour for each ingredient: white for dairy, yellow for cooked food, blue for raw fish, red for raw meat, green for vegetables.

Colander A large bowl with lots of holes in it. It is used for draining water from food.

Fish slice This is a long, flat piece of equipment with slits in which is often used for turning food in a frying pan or for serving fish.

Garlic crusher This is a gadget with two handles used for squashing garlic into small pieces.

Knives You don't really need a lot of different knives – just two or three good ones. Always take care when handling knives and ask a grown-up to help.

Measuring scales You'll need these to weigh out ingredients correctly.

Pastry brush This is a brush used to glaze things like pies before baking.

Rolling pin A cylinder with handles at each end used to roll out dough and pastry until it is flat and thin.

Sieve A utensil with a bottom covered in lots of tiny holes. We use a sieve for sifting and straining, it is often used to remove lumps from flour.

Spatula A utensil with a flexible rounded end. A spatula can be used for lots of tasks such as folding, mixing and scraping.

Spoons There are three spoons which are often used in recipes to measure things. The smallest is a teaspoon (5 ml), a dessertspoon (10 ml) is the middle-sized spoon and is the spoon you would use to eat a pudding or cereal. A tablespoon (15 ml) is the largest spoon. You might use this spoon to serve food. Wooden spoons are used for stirring and mixing things like sauces and fillings.

Saucepans and frying pans Most kitchens will have a selection of pans in different sizes.

Whisk A utensil made of looped wires which are joined at the handle. It is often used to beat eggs.

a balanced diet

In order to keep our bodies healthy and working properly we must eat the right amounts of a range of different foods. This is called a balanced diet.

There are five different types of foods, or food groups. They are:
• fruits and vegetables
• carbohydrates
• protein
• dairy
• salt, fat and sugary foods.

To stay healthy when you are growing you should eat lots of fruit and vegetables and lots of carbohydrates, some protein and some dairy. Try and keep salt, fats and sugary food for a treat. The diagram opposite shows a 'plate' with the corrrect proportions of food from each food group.

Why eat a balanced diet?
Eating a balanced diet can help you to stay healthy and active. The food groups have different effects on your body.
• **Fruits and vegetables** contain vitamins and minerals to stop you from getting ill and fibre to keep you clean on the inside.
• **Carbohydrates** are a great source of 'slow-release' energy. They help keep you going through all your favourite activities.
• **Protein** helps your body to grow and repair itself.
• **Dairy** contains calcium, which can keep your bones, hair, teeth and nails healthy.
• **Salt, fat, sugar** should be eaten as occasional treats. Try eating dried or fresh fruit for an energy filled snack, which contain natural sugar.

fruits and vegetables   carbohydrates

protein   dairy

salt, fat, sugar

Food groups and healthy proportions

top tips for healthy bodies
• Eat at least 5 portions of fruit and vegetables each day. A portion is roughly about as big as your fist. Aim for 3 vegetables and 2 fruits.
• Drink enough water. Our bodies are made up of at least 70% water. Water also helps you to concentrate so replace those fizzy drinks with water.
• Take plenty of regular exercise.

tips and techniques

Sometimes when following a recipe, you might come across a word or an instruction that you haven't seen before or that you don't understand. Some of these might be 'culinary terms' which are words that are specific to cookery and food. Here are some common culinary terms to help you with your cooking.

Bake blind To cook a pastry case without any filling in it.

Bring to the boil To put a saucepan of water on to a hob until it starts to bubble.

Drain To separate liquid from food when cooked. The easiest way to do this is with a colander.

Flake To break into small pieces.

Grease To spread some kind of fat (often butter) over the inside of a pan or tin to stop food from sticking during cooking.

Knead To stretch, fold and press a dough over and over again (usually with your hands) until it becomes smooth and stretchy.

Line To cover the bottom and sides of tins with baking paper. We often have to do this when baking cakes as it stops the cake sticking to the tin.

Pinch Often used to describe an amount of salt. It is as much as you can hold between your thumb and pointing finger.

Simmer To keep a pan of liquid at just below the boiling point. Heat the liquid until tiny bubbles rise to the surface. If big bubbles start to appear this means the liquid is boiling and you will need to reduce the heat.

Top and tail Removing both ends of a vegetable.

some tips and techniques

- If you are measuring liquid, put the measuring jug on a flat surface so that you get an accurate measurement. When using measuring scales, make sure you are looking straight at the display to get an accurate reading.
- When chopping onions, your eyes might start to water. Never rub your eyes when this happens as it will make it worse. If it gets too bad, try putting your wrists under cold running water.
- When breaking raw eggs, never break the shell on the side of the bowl you are using as pieces of shell could fall in. Tap the widest part of the egg on a work surface.
- It is not always necessary to add salt to food. A healthier way to make food tasty is by adding different herbs and spices.

breakfast

Breakfast doesn't have to be the same boring thing every day. These are some of my favourite breakfast dishes – and they are high in carbohydrates. Cereals, grains and bread are all foods which will give you energy for your day ahead. Try livening up your breakfast with some fruit and make a start with your five-a-day target.

creamy scrambled eggs

Eggs are an excellent source of protein and the toast will give you lots of energy to start the day. This dish is delicious for breakfast, but you can eat it any time of day!

SERVES **2** • PREPARATION TIME: **5 MINUTES** • COOKING TIME: **10–12 MINUTES**

SHOPPING LIST

- 4 eggs
- 100 ml (4 fl oz/½ cup) milk
- A knob of butter
- Pinch of salt and pepper
- 2 tsp double (heavy) cream
- buttered toast, to serve

whisking the eggs

you will also need

Mixing bowl, whisk, measuring jug, saucepan, wooden spoon, teaspoon

Assemble all the ingredients and equipment you need. Make sure you understand what everything is, especially anything you haven't used before. Wash your hands and put on a clean apron.

buttering the toast

" I love cracking **eggs** and can even do it without breaking the **yolk**! **"** JAMIE, 7

1 Carefully break the eggs into a mixing bowl. Using the whisk, beat the eggs well until they are light and frothy.

2 Pour the eggs into the saucepan. Add the milk, butter, salt and pepper and stir together with the wooden spoon.

3 Put the saucepan over a low heat and keep stirring until the eggs start to cook and 'scramble' into pieces. Make sure you get the wooden spoon into the edges of the pan so the egg does not burn.

4 When the egg mixture no longer looks runny, remove from the heat and add the cream. Mix well and serve on hot buttered toast.

cereal
mixed with fruit

Cereal doesn't need to be boring – and with this simple recipe there's no excuse. Mix up different grains and fruits each day in your cereal. You can use dried and fresh fruit, depending on what is available.

SERVES **1** • PREPARATION TIME: **5 MINUTES**

SHOPPING LIST

• 2 large ripe strawberries

• A few blueberries

• A few raspberries

• 2–3 tbsp mixed cereal (e.g. cornflakes or branflakes)

• 100 ml (4 fl oz/½ cup) full fat milk

adding fruit to the cereal

you will also need

Small bowl, tablespoon, chopping board, round ended knife

Assemble all the ingredients and equipment you will need. Make sure you understand what everything is, especially anything you haven't used before. Wash your hands and put on a clean apron.

did you know? Breakfast is the most important meal of the day – children who eat breakfast concentrate better in lessons. Nuts are a good source of protein and energy.

1 Select and mix your chosen cereals in a small bowl.

2 Wash the strawberries and remove the stalks. Carefully chop them into bite-size pieces. Add them to the cereal with the raspberries and blueberries and mix well.

3 Add milk and serve.

variations You can use almost any fruit for this recipe, including fresh fruits or dried fruits such as apricots and sultanas. Add some chopped nuts for extra crunch.

" I like **cereal** because it gives me lots of **energy** until lunchtime! " **ABIGAIL, 7**

fruit cocktail

This is a great way of adding extra zest to fruit juice.

SERVES **4** • PREPARATION TIME: **10 MINUTES**

SHOPPING LIST

• 4 oranges (approx 400 ml (14 fl oz/ 1½ cups) when squeezed)

• 500 ml (17 fl oz/2 cups) fresh apple juice

• ½ lime or ½ grapefruit

• 1–2 tsp sugar (optional)

squeezing the orange juice

you will also need

Chopping board, sharp knife, lemon squeezer, measuring jug, serving jug, tall glass

Assemble all the ingredients and equipment you need. Make sure you understand what everything is, especially anything you haven't used before. Wash your hands and put on a clean apron.

tips If you have a juicer at home you can make up your own juice by using fruits like mangoes, apples, pineapples, bananas, berries. If you roll citrus fruits on a surface with the palm of your hand, you get much more juice out of the fruit when you squeeze them.

66 This makes an **awesome** drink, but you can also **freeze** it for ice lollies! 99 **SAM, 10**

1 Carefully cut the oranges and lime or grapefruit in half and squeeze the juice from the fruit using the lemon squeezer.

2 Pour the apple juice into the serving jug and add your freshly squeezed fruit juice to this. Taste to see if you need to add sugar. Put the mixed juice into the fridge to chill before serving.

3 Serve in tall glasses over ice.

banana and mango smoothie

Smoothies are bursting with vitamins and minerals to keep you healthy and full of energy for the day ahead. They are also great to serve at parties and when friends come round, instead of sugary fizzy drinks.

SERVES **2–4** • PREPARATION TIME: **15 MINUTES**

SHOPPING LIST

- 175 g (6 oz) mango (you can use raspberries or strawberries instead)
- 1 ripe banana
- 100–150 ml (4–5 fl oz/½ cup) whole milk
- 100 ml (4 fl oz/½ cup) Greek or natural yoghurt
- 1 tbsp honey (optional)

you will also need

Measuring scales, measuring jug, chopping board, sharp knife, tablespoon, blender

slicing the mango

Assemble all the ingredients and equipment you need. Make sure you understand what everything is, especially anything you haven't used before. Wash your hands and put on a clean apron.

1 If using mango, cut two large slices of mango either side of the stone and scoop out the flesh. Ease away the rest of the flesh from around the stone using the knife or spoon. Chop the mango flesh into pieces and discard the skin.

2 Peel and slice the banana. If you are using berries, remove any stalks or leaves.

3 Put the fruit into the blender and add the yoghurt and milk.

4 Add the honey, if using. Put on the lid and liquidise until smooth.

measuring out the milk

scooping out the mango flesh

whizzing the smoothie in the blender

pancakes

Pancakes are fun and quick to make and are a great weekend breakfast treat. Experiment with sweet and savoury fillings to impress your family and friends.

MAKES ABOUT **6–8 PANCAKES** • PREPARATION TIME: **15 MINUTES** • COOKING TIME: **15 MINUTES**

SHOPPING LIST

- 225 g (8 oz/2¼ cups) plain (all-purpose) flour
- Pinch of salt
- 2 eggs
- 300 ml (10 fl oz/1¼ cups) milk
- 2 tbsp oil
- To serve: lemon juice and sugar or fresh fruit

you will also need

2 mixing bowls, sieve, whisk or fork, frying pan, ladle, fish slice or spatula, measuring jug

breaking the eggs into a bowl

Assemble all the ingredients and equipment you need. Make sure you understand what everything is, especially anything you haven't used before. Wash your hands and put on a clean apron.

1 Break the eggs into a separate mixing bowl and beat them with a whisk or fork. Stir in the milk.

2 Sift the flour into a large mixing bowl. Add a small pinch of salt.

sifting the flour into a
bowl

pouring batter into the
pan

4 Heat 1 teaspoon of oil in a frying pan over a medium/high heat. Once the oil and the pan are hot, carefully pour or spoon (using the ladle) some of the batter into the centre of the pan.

5 Tilt the pan in a circular motion so the batter spreads and covers the base of the pan with a thin, even layer.

6 Allow the pancake to brown on one side for about 3 minutes. Make sure you give the pancake time to cook and don't turn it over too early!

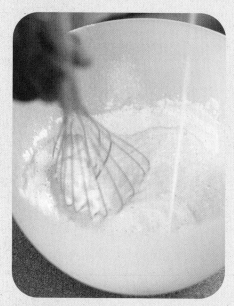

whisking the milk and
egg mixture into the flour

3 Add the milk and egg mixture to the flour very slowly. Beat well with the whisk and make sure all the flour is incorporated into the mixture. Keep beating until the mixture is smooth and has no lumps in it.

turning the pancake over

Tossing pancakes is so much **fun**! **LARA, 13**

7 Using a fish slice or spatula, loosen the edges of the pancake from the pan and then toss or turn the pancake over on to the other side. Cook the second side for a further minute. Each pancake will vary in its cooking time depending on the thickness of the batter and the heat of the pan. Don't worry if your first pancake sticks as this often happens!

8 Keep making pancakes until all the batter is used up, adding just half a teaspoon of oil before you start each one. You can keep the cooked pancakes warm by wrapping in a clean tea towel while you cook the rest.

9 Serve the pancakes with a squeeze of fresh lemon juice and a sprinkling of sugar or some fresh fruit (strawberries, raspberries and blueberries all work brilliantly).

extra ideas For a more substantial breakfast, try filling the pancakes with grated cheese, spinach, ham or mushrooms.

25

healthy snacks and lovely lunchboxes

Don't follow the crowd at lunchtime; try something a little different. With these tasty snacks you will be the envy of all your friends. If you need a quick and easy snack on-the-go then try one of these instead of reaching for crisps or chocolate. Many of these yummy dishes can be eaten warm or left to cool to take to school or on a picnic.

cheesy bread rolls

These are delicious and because you make them yourself there are no additives. They can be made in advance and put in lunch boxes or taken out on a picnic.

MAKES **8–10 ROLLS** • PREPARATION TIME: **UP TO 1½ HOURS** • COOKING TIME: **20–25 MINUTES**

SHOPPING LIST

- 50 g (2 oz) butter or margarine
- 150 ml (5 fl oz/¾ cup) milk
- 450 g (1 lb/4½ cups) strong plain (all-purpose) flour, plus extra for dusting
- 1 tsp caster (superfine) sugar
- small pinch of salt
- small pinch of mustard powder
- 1 tbsp fast-action dried yeast
- 1 egg
- 100 g (4 oz/¾ cup) Cheddar cheese
- 3 tbsp milk or beaten egg for glazing

you will also need

Baking tray, greaseproof paper, measuring scales, measuring jug, small saucepan, sieve, large mixing bowl, wooden spoon, small mixing bowl, fork, cheese grater, clingfilm or tea towel, round-ended knife, pastry brush, cooling rack

Assemble all the ingredients and equipment you will need. Make sure you understand what everything is, especially anything you haven't used before. Wash your hands and put on a clean apron.

making a well in the flour

1 Preheat the oven to 220°C (425°F/ Gas mark 7). Grease the baking tray or line it with greaseproof paper.

2 Put the butter and milk in a small pan over a low heat and cook until the butter has melted. Remove from the heat and allow to cool.

3 Sift the flour into a large mixing bowl. Add the sugar, salt, mustard powder and yeast and mix.

grating the cheese

mixing to make a dough

66 If you make it **yourself** it is much more **yummy**! **99**

DAISY, 9

4 Crack the egg into a small mixing bowl and beat well with a fork. Make a well in the flour and add the beaten egg, then add the melted butter and warm milk. Mix well.

did you know? Yeast is actually a fungus. When it is mixed with warm liquid and flour it grows quickly, making the bread rise.

5 Grate the cheese and add to the mixing bowl. Mix really well until everything comes together to form a fairly soft dough that leaves the sides of the bowl clean (you can do this with your hands if it gets too difficult to do with a wooden spoon). If the dough is too sticky, add some more flour and if it is too dry, add some more milk.

kneading the dough

shaping the dough into balls

6 Turn the dough out on to a work surface or board that is dusted with flour. Knead well for 5 minutes or until the dough is smooth and no longer sticky.

7 Put your dough back into the bowl and cover with cling film or a clean tea towel. Leave the dough in a warm place (such as an airing cupboard) to allow the yeast to act until you have a ball of dough that has increased in size and feels light and 'airy' to the touch. This could take anything from 15 minutes to 1 hour.

8 When the dough is ready, turn it back out on to the floured surface and knead lightly. Divide the dough into 8–10 equal sized pieces.

9 Shape each piece into a round bun and place on the lined baking tray. Leave plenty of room between as they will get bigger as they bake.

10 Glaze the top of your rolls by brushing them with milk or beaten egg.

brushing the tops with milk

11 Bake in the middle of the oven for 20–25 minutes. Cooking time will vary depending on the size of the rolls.

12 Remove from the oven and allow to cool on a wire cooling rack.

vegetable sticks with avocado dip

When you're hungry and need a quick bite reach for a healthy snack. Use a wide variety of crunchy and colourful vegetables to liven up your lunchbox.

SERVES **2–3** • PREPARATION TIME: **20 MINUTES**

SHOPPING LIST

For the vegetable sticks:

- 2 celery sticks
- 1 pepper (whichever colour is your favourite)
- 10 sugar snap (snow) peas
- 6 baby corn
- 2 carrots

For the avocado dip:

- 1 garlic clove
- 2–3 ripe avocados (approx. 500 g/ 18 oz)
- 1 tbsp lemon juice
- 2 tbsp cream cheese
- pinch of salt and pepper
- Few drops of chilli sauce or a pinch of paprika (optional)

you will also need

Vegetable peeler, sharp knife, chopping board, dessert spoon, mixing bowl, lemon squeezer, fork, serving bowl and plate

Assemble all the ingredients and equipment you will need. Make sure you understand what everything is, especially anything you haven't used before. Wash your hands and put on a clean apron.

did you know? An avocado is a fruit because it has a stone in the middle. It's high in protein and oil and is really good for you.

peeling celery with a vegetable peeler

31

1 First wash the celery, peppers, sugar snap (snow) peas and baby corn. Peel the carrots and celery and remove the seeds from the pepper. Carefully cut these vegetables into strips. You can eat sugar snap (snow) peas and baby corn whole.

2 Split the avocados in half. You can do this by carefully cutting down the middle of the avocado until you reach the stone. Cut all the way round the stone. Twist the avocado and turn until the two halves can be pulled apart. Remove the stone.

3 Using the spoon, scoop out the green flesh avocado into the mixing bowl.

4 Peel and crush or chop the garlic and set aside.

slicing into the avocado

twisting the avocado to separate the halves

cutting the red pepper into strips

crushing the garlic clove

66 I like making this **colourful** snack for my **lunchbox** 99   SANDY, 8

5 Add the garlic, lemon juice, cream cheese, and, if using, a few drops of chilli sauce or a pinch of paprika to the avocado. Using a fork, mash everything to a smooth pulp.

6 Season the mixture with salt and pepper to taste.

7 Put the dip into a serving bowl and put this on a plate with the vegetable sticks.

spring rolls

These spring rolls are cooked in the oven which makes them healthier and less fatty than the ones you find at takeaways. Spring rolls are usually filled with lightly cooked spring vegetables but they can also contain meat.

MAKES **4** • PREPARATION TIME: **25 MINUTES** • COOKING TIME: **20–25 MINUTES**

SHOPPING LIST

- 1 garlic clove
- 50 g (2 oz/⅓ cup) white onion
- 150 g (5 oz) carrots
- ½ red pepper
- 2 spring onions (scallions)
- 50 g (2 oz) white cabbage
- ½ tsp ginger, peeled and chopped
- 75 g (3 oz) beansprouts
- 40 g (1½ oz) fine rice/stir fry noodles
- Approximately 500 ml (18 fl oz/ 2 cups) boiling water
- 3 tbsp sesame, groundnut, vegetable or olive oil
- 1 tbsp light soy sauce
- 8 sheets filo pastry (cover with a damp tea towel until needed)
- Water for brushing

you will also need

Vegetable peeler, chopping board, sharp knife, mixing bowl, heatproof mixing bowl or jug, colander, wooden spoon, wok or large saucepan, pastry brush, greaseproof paper, baking tray

Assemble all the ingredients and equipment you need. Make sure you understand what everything is, especially anything you haven't used before. Wash your hands and put on a clean apron.

cutting the red pepper into strips

66 These are **fun** to make and taste **yummy**! 99 SARA, 7

1 Preheat the oven to 190°C (375°F/Gas mark 5). Peel and finely chop the garlic and onion. Cut the carrot and red pepper into strips. Finely chop the spring onions (scallions) and finely shred the cabbage. Put all of these into the mixing bowl along with chopped ginger and the beansprouts and mix together.

2 Put the noodles into the heatproof mixing bowl or jug and cover with the boiling water. Allow to soak for approximately 5 minutes, stirring occasionally to separate the noodles. Drain using the colander and return to the bowl/jug. Set aside to allow to cool.

3 Heat 2 tbsp oil in a wok or large saucepan over a high heat until the oil is very hot. Carefully put all of the vegetables into the wok and stir-fry for 2 minutes until softened and partly cooked.

4 Add the soy sauce and cook for a further 1 minute. Remove from the heat. Roughly chop the noodles, add to the vegetables and mix well. Allow this to cool.

5 Lay out a sheet of filo pastry and lightly brush around the edges with water. Fold in half so the brushed edges stick together.

6 Place a quarter of the mixture on to the pastry in a line. Fold the edges in at the side – this stops the mixture falling out. Roll the edge of the pastry over the filling and continue rolling until you get to the end. Press the end lightly to seal. Repeat for the other three spring rolls.

7 Line a baking tray with greaseproof paper and place the rolls on to this. Brush the top of the rolls with a little oil to make them crispy.

8 Bake in the preheated oven for 20–25 minutes or until golden brown and crispy.

brushing the edges of the pastry with water

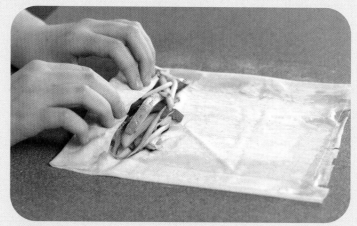

starting to roll

folding the edges of the pastry in

keep rolling!

potato and bean salad

Not just an old fashioned potato salad: this dish contains beans which are an important source of protein for vegetarians.

SERVES **4** • PREPARATION TIME: **20 MINUTES** • COOKING TIME: **10–15 MINUTES**

SHOPPING LIST

- 4 medium potatoes
- 50 g (2 oz) French beans
- 50 g (2 oz) sweetcorn
- 50 g (2 oz) kidney or butter beans
- 4 spring onions (scallions) (optional)
- 2 tsp chopped fresh herbs e.g. parsley, chives, coriander (cilantro)
- 5 tbsp mayonnaise
- Salt and pepper
- Pinch of paprika
- Pinch of curry powder

Assemble all the ingredients and equipment you need. Make sure you understand what everything is, especially anything you haven't used before. Wash your hands and put on a clean apron.

variations

- Add your favourite ingredients to the basic potato salad eg: tuna fish, chopped crispy bacon, chopped salami, button mushrooms
- Try adding a crushed garlic clove to the mayonnaise for a different flavour

you will also need

Vegetable peeler, chopping board, sharp knife, 2 saucepans with lids, timer, tin opener, colander or sieve, round-ended knife, tablespoon, small mixing bowl, salad bowl and servers, wooden spoon

peeling potatoes

cutting the cooked potato into chunks

slicing spring onions

1 Carefully peel the potatoes and cut them into even bite-sized pieces. Put the potatoes into a saucepan of cold water. Add a pinch of salt and put the pan over a medium heat until the water comes to the boil. At boiling point, turn the heat down and allow the potatoes to simmer gently until they are cooked. (The time will vary depending on the type and size of the potatoes, but will take approximately 10–15 minutes.)

2 While the potatoes are cooking, top and tail the French beans. Wash them well and place them in a saucepan of boiling water. Add a pinch of salt and cook for 5–7 minutes (again the cooking time may change as with all fresh vegetables). Be careful that you do not cook them too much. They should be soft but still have a 'bite' to them.

3 While you are waiting for the potatoes and beans to cook, carefully open the tins of sweetcorn and kidney/butter beans. Drain off any excess liquid from the sweetcorn. Rinse the kidney/butter beans under cold water and then leave them to drain.

4 Check the French beans and potatoes and see if they are cooked. When they are ready, drain them well through a colander. Run some cold water over the beans. This stops them from cooking any further and will refresh them so they stay a bright green colour.

5 If you are using spring onions (scallions) in your salad, wash them well and chop them into small slices. Wash the herbs and chop them finely. Place the spring onions (scallions) and herbs in your large salad serving bowl. Save some of the herbs for garnish later.

6 Spoon the mayonnaise into the small mixing bowl. Add a pinch of salt and pepper and mix well.

7 Add the potatoes and French beans to the spring onions (scallions) and herbs in your salad bowl. Next add the drained sweetcorn and kidney/butter beans and mix everything well. Add the mayonnaise and toss well using a spoon until all the ingredients are coated. Cover and chill your salad in the fridge until you are ready to eat it.

8 Garnish your salad with the herbs you set aside earlier and serve.

adding mayonnaise and mixing through

handy hint Potatoes are a great source of carbohydrate and provide our bodies with lots of good energy.

fresh fruit kebabs

These fresh fruit kebabs are a really healthy snack when you need something sweet and juicy. You can make some lovely colourful combinations by mixing up different fruit. They are best eaten within half an hour of making them so the fruit doesn't discolour.

SERVES **4** • PREPARATION TIME: **25 MINUTES**

SHOPPING LIST

• 450 g (1 lb) fresh fruit in season, such as strawberries, raspberries, blackberries, kiwi, mango, apples, pears, bananas, seedless grapes, pineapple

you will also need

Sharp knife, colander, chopping board, vegetable peeler, wooden skewers or cocktail sticks

Assemble all the ingredients and equipment you need. Make sure you understand what everything is, especially anything you haven't used before. Wash your hands and put on a clean apron.

tip Always choose fruits that are bright in colour and have no bruises – they will be fresher and taste better.

1 Assemble the fresh fruit you have chosen.

2 Carefully cut the top off the strawberries and remove grapes from the stalks. Place these fruits in the colander along with any others that do not need to be peeled (i.e. blackberries and raspberries). Wash the fruits with cold running water and leave to drain.

3 If you are using pineapple, peel it carefully and remove the sharp points. Cut the flesh into bite-sized pieces. You can use tinned pineapple if you can't find fresh pineapple.

4 Peel the kiwi, mango and banana and cut into bite size pieces.

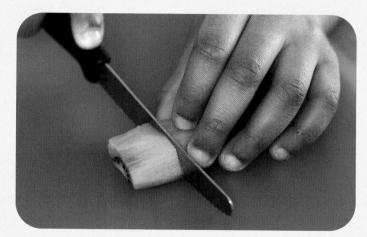

cutting up a kiwi fruit

threading the fruit onto skewers

5 Cut the apples and pears into quarters and remove the cores. Cut into bite-sized pieces.

6 Thread the pieces of fruit onto the skewers one at a time. Vary the order of the fruit to make the kebabs nice and colourful. Make sure the fruit is tightly packed so it stays on the sticks.

pitta pockets

This is a great snack for when you are on the go – carry a whole meal in your hand!
We've used cooked chicken here but you could also fill the pockets with tuna or grated
cheese.

SERVES **4–6** • PREPARATION TIME: *15 MINUTES*

SHOPPING LIST

- 4–6 pitta breads
- 2 spring onions (scallions)
- 50 g (2 oz) cucumber
- 8 baby tomatoes
- 250 g (9 oz) cooked chicken
- 4–5 lettuce leaves, shredded
- ½ red pepper, sliced
- 2 tbsp mayonnaise

you will also need

Chopping board, sharp knife, mixing bowl,
2 tablespoons, measuring scales

Assemble all the ingredients and equipment you
need. Make sure you understand what everything is,
especially anything you haven't used before. Wash
your hands and put on a clean apron.

1 Cut one edge off each of the pitta breads so it
makes an opening into the bread. This is so that
you will be able to push the chosen filling down into
the bread pocket.

slicing open the pitta bread

2 Slice the spring onions (scallions), cucumber and half the tomatoes and put into the mixing bowl. Cut the chicken and add to the bowl along with the lettuce, and sliced pepper. Mix everything together.

3 Spread the mayonnaise inside the pitta breads and then stuff the breads with the chicken and salad mix.

filling the pitta pocket

handy hint Did you know that brown bread is better for you than white bread? This is because brown bread has more fibre, which is essential for a healthy gut.

43

warm pasta salad

A pasta salad with a difference. This is delicious as an after-school snack or you can let it cool down and pack some in your lunchbox.

SERVES **2–4** • PREPARATION TIME: **20 MINUTES** • COOKING TIME: **15 MINUTES**

SHOPPING LIST

- 300 g (10 oz/2½ cups) pasta
- 2 tbsp olive oil
- Pinch of salt
- 150 g (5 oz) of any of the following: pancetta, salami, cooked bacon bits, cooked chicken, pepperoni (any cooked meat can be used)
- ½ onion, peeled and chopped
- 1 garlic clove, peeled and chopped or crushed
- 50 g (2 oz) peppers, chopped (any colours are fine)
- 2 tbsp sweetcorn
- 50 g (2 oz) baby tomatoes, quartered
- 2 tbsp peas
- 2 spring onions (scallions), chopped
- 3 tbsp chopped fresh herbs (e.g. parsley, basil or chives)
- 200 ml (7 fl oz/¾ cup) cream
- 50 g (2 oz/½ cup) grated cheese (cheddar or parmesan)

you will also need

2 large saucepans, colander, wooden spoon, chopping board, sharp knife

Assemble all the ingredients and equipment you need. Make sure you understand what everything is, especially anything you haven't used before. Wash your hands and put on a clean apron.

pouring boiling water onto the pasta

1 Put the pasta into a large saucepan with 1 tbsp olive oil and a pinch of salt. Add enough boiling water to the pan to cover the pasta. Set over a medium heat and cook according to the packet instructions. When the pasta is cooked, drain using the colander.

using a tin opener

draining the pasta

chopping fresh parsley

2 Heat 1 tbsp oil in a large pan and add the cooked meat. Cook gently for 1–2 minutes. Add the onion, garlic and peppers and cook for a further minute.

3 Reduce the heat to low. Add the sweetcorn, tomatoes, peas, spring onions (scallions), herbs and the cream. Cook for 1–2 minutes or until the cream has thickened.

4 Add the cooked pasta and then increase the heat. Cook, stirring, for about one minute.

5 Remove from the heat, sprinkle the cheese over the top and serve immediately. Alternatively, let it cool down and take some to school in your lunchbox.

did you know? that a red pepper is a superfood? This means that it is full of nutrients and is very good for your body and keeps you healthy. Just half a red pepper will provide you with enough vitamin C for one day.

spanish omelette

A traditional Spanish omelette contains potatoes as well as eggs. The herbs add great flavour to the dish. You can eat this omelette hot or warm but is also delicious cold – perfect for picnics or packed lunches!

SERVES **4** • PREPARATION TIME: **30 MINUTES** • COOKING TIME: **10–15 MINUTES**

SHOPPING LIST

- 6 eggs
- 1 tbsp fresh chopped herbs (eg oregano, chives)
- Salt and pepper
- 1 medium onion
- ½ red or yellow pepper
- 100 g (4 oz/½ cup) potatoes, peeled and cooked
- 1 garlic clove
- 1 tbsp olive oil
- 50–75 g (2–3 oz/½ cup) grated cheese
- Chopped chives, to garnish

you will also need

Measuring scales, chopping board, colander, whisk, sharp knife, mixing bowl, large frying pan, wooden spoon, vegetable peeler, cheese grater

Assemble all the ingredients and equipment you need. Make sure you understand what everything is, especially anything you haven't used before. Wash your hands and put on a clean apron.

why don't you try? You could also add chorizo (a spicy Spanish sausage), cooked bacon, cooked sausage, ham, cooked chicken, sweetcorn, peas or tomatoes.

chopping onion

1 Crack the eggs into a small bowl and whisk them. Add the herbs to the egg and season with a pinch of salt and pepper.

2 Peel and dice the onion. Dice the pepper, slice the potatoes and peel and chop the garlic.

cooking the onion, garlic, pepper and potatoes

slicing the cooked potato

3 Heat the olive oil in a large frying pan over a high heat. Add the potatoes and fry until lightly golden, turning occasionally. This should take between 1 and 2 minutes. Add the onion, garlic, and peppers and cook for a further 1–2 minutes.

adding the eggs to the pan

4 Pour the egg mixture into the pan over the vegetables. Reduce the heat to low and cook for 2–3 minutes. Add any of the optional extras you are using and sprinkle the grated cheese over the top. Turn on the grill to a medium heat.

5 Once the egg mixture is almost set, place the pan under the grill for 3–4 minutes or until golden brown. Check the egg is cooked and not runny. Serve hot or cold, garnished with chives.

putting the omelette under the grill

work it out! This recipe uses foods from every food group. The five food groups are: Fruit and Vegetables; Carbohydrates; Protein; Dairy and Fat, Salt and Sugar. Which groups would the following ingredients fit into: pepper, potato, cheese?

family weekend meals

It's always fun to cook for other people and it's great to sit down and enjoy a homemade meal together. These dishes will take a little longer to prepare but I can promise that it will be worth it. Make sure you get some help with the washing up!

roast chicken

This is a traditional meal for a Sunday lunch. It's also great enjoyed at a family celebration. The chicken is cooked in the oven and will fill the house with an irresistible smell!

SERVES **4–6** • PREPARATION TIME: **30 MINUTES** • COOKING TIME: **AT LEAST 1 HOUR 20 MINUTES**

SHOPPING LIST

• 1 lemon

• 75 g (3 oz) butter

• 2 garlic cloves, crushed

• Salt and pepper

• 1 tsp chopped thyme

• 1 chicken (see note, opposite)

• Approx 300 g (10 oz) parsnips

• Approx 350 g (11 oz) carrots

• Approx 350 g (11 oz) potatoes

note This recipe is based on a 1.5-kg (3-lb) chicken which will serve 4–6 people. Cooking times do vary but as a guideline it is 20 minutes per 500 g (1 lb) plus an additional 20 minutes until the chicken is cooked thoroughly.

using oven gloves

you will also need

Sharp knife, chopping board, measuring scales, garlic crusher, small mixing bowl, teaspoon, roasting tray, vegetable peeler, tablespoon

Assemble all the ingredients and equipment you need. Make sure you understand what everything is, especially anything you haven't used before. Wash your hands and put on a clean apron.

1 Preheat the oven to 180°C (350°F/Gas mark 4). Carefully cut the lemon in half and push inside the chicken. Put the butter, crushed garlic, a pinch of salt and pepper and the chopped thyme into a small mixing bowl. Mix everything together with a teaspoon. Use your hands to spread the mixture all over the top of the chicken so it is well coated.

66 In my **family** we all help with the **roast** dinner which is lots of **fun**! 99 DENZEL, 11

2 Put the chicken on to a large roasting tray and put into the preheated oven to start cooking for 20 minutes (in total the chicken will take approximately 1 hour 20 minutes to cook).

3 While the chicken is starting to cook, peel the parsnips, carrots and potatoes and carefully cut them into wedge shapes. Some vegetables, like the carrots, can be left whole.

adding the vegetables to the roasting tray

4 After the chicken has been cooking for about 20 minutes you should remove it from the oven (make sure you use oven gloves, it will be very hot!) and carefully baste the chicken with its own juices. Baste means to spoon the juices that have run from the chicken during cooking over the top of the chicken. This stops the chicken from drying out and gives it more flavour. You should repeat this process every 20–30 minutes while the chicken is cooking.

6 The cooking times of the chicken and the vegetables will vary depending on their size. When a chicken is cooked it is white in the very middle.

carving the chicken (get an adult to help!)

basting the chicken

5 Put the vegetable wedges into the roasting tray around the chicken. Return the chicken to the oven to cook for approximately 1 more hour, basting half way through.

handy hint roasting is a very economical way of cooking as you can put everything into the oven together. The meat goes in with all the vegetables – and it tastes great too!
Always wash and dry hands thoroughly after touching raw chicken.

kedgeree

If you haven't eaten much fish before, this is a great way to start, as it is mixed with lots of rice and other ingredients. The spices add some lovely interesting flavours.

SERVES 2–4 • **PREPARATION TIME: 25 MINUTES** • **COOKING TIME: 25 MINUTES**

SHOPPING LIST

- 200 g (7 oz/1 cup) rice
- 4 eggs
- 3 tbsp chopped fresh coriander (cilantro)
- 500 g (18 oz) boneless and skinless cod, salmon or haddock
- Zest of 1 lime
- 1 tbsp olive oil
- 1 medium onion, peeled and chopped
- 1½ tsp garlic, peeled and chopped
- 1 tsp chopped ginger
- 1 tsp curry powder
- ¼ tsp turmeric
- 1 tsp ground cumin
- ½ tsp ground coriander
- 200 ml (7 fl oz/¾ cup) double (heavy) cream
- Salt and pepper

you will also need

Measuring scales, mixing bowl, colander, 3 saucepans, kettle, mixing bowl, measuring jug, chopping board, sharp knife

Assemble all the ingredients and equipment you need. Make sure you understand what everything is, especially anything you haven't used before. Wash your hands and put on a clean apron.

washing the rice in cold water

1 Wash the rice thoroughly and leave to soak in a saucepan for 10 minutes. Drain and then cook according to the instructions on the packet. Drain the rice and set aside.

2 Put the eggs into a saucepan, cover with boiling water and cook for 10 minutes. Run the pan under cold water until the eggs are cool. Peel and roughly chop the eggs and put into a mixing bowl with the chopped coriander (cilantro).

peeling the hardboiled eggs

3 Place the fish into a large saucepan with 300 ml (10 fl oz/1¼ cup) water or enough to half-cover the fish. Bring the water to a simmer and gently poach the fish for 10 minutes over a low to medium heat. Allow the fish to cool slightly and then drain but make sure you keep the water (stock) that the fish was cooked in as you will need it later.

4 When the fish is cool enough, gently break it into flakes making sure you check for any bones. Add the flaked fish to the bowl with the eggs and add the lime zest.

flaking the cooked fish

5 In a large clean saucepan, heat 1 tbsp olive oil and fry the onion, garlic and ginger for 1–2 minutes over a medium heat until soft and light in colour. Add the spices to the pan and cook for another minute.

6 Add 300 ml (10 fl oz/1¼ cup) of the reserved fish stock. If you don't have enough fish stock you can top it up with water. Bring to the boil for 1–2 minutes, reduce the heat and add the cream. Simmer for 2–3 minutes.

7 Add the rice and then the fish and egg mixture. Gently warm through and mix. Check the seasoning and if required add a pinch of salt and pepper.

adding the cooked rice to the pan

“ I like **fish** because it tastes **good** and makes you **brainy**! AMY, 9

shepherd's pie

This dish used to be made with leftovers from a roast lamb. You can make this version from scratch for a tasty family supper. Serve with some fresh green vegetables for a lovely balanced meal.

SERVES **4** • PREPARATION TIME: **20 MINUTES** • COOKING TIME: **45 MINUTES**

SHOPPING LIST

- 700 g (1½ lb oz) potatoes
- Salt and pepper
- 1 tbsp olive oil
- 500 g (18 oz) minced lamb (or beef)
- 2 cloves garlic, crushed or chopped
- 2 medium onions, peeled and chopped
- 1 stick celery, chopped
- 1 small carrot, peeled and chopped or grated
- 3 tbsp leeks, chopped
- 1 tsp thyme, chopped
- ½ tbsp tomato purée
- ½ tbsp Worcestershire sauce
- 1–2 beef stock cubes
- 1 tbsp butter
- 4 tbsp milk
- 75 g (3 oz/¾ cup) grated cheese (optional)

you will also need

Measuring scales, chopping board, mixing bowl, large frying pan, sharp knife, potato masher, tablespoon, wooden spoon, ovenproof dish, medium saucepan, vegetable peeler, colander, cheese grater

Assemble all the ingredients and equipment you need. Make sure you understand what everything is, especially anything you haven't used before. Wash your hands and put on a clean apron.

cooking the mince

1 Preheat the oven to 190°C (375°F/Gas mark 5). Peel and chop the potatoes into equal sizes and put them in a medium saucepan. Add a pinch of salt and cover with cold water. Cover the saucepan with a lid and place on a medium heat to cook until tender.

2 While the potatoes are cooking, heat the olive oil in a large frying pan. Add the mince and stir to 'break' it down using a wooden spoon. Cook the mince for 2–3 minutes over a high heat until it is brown all over.

other ideas You can add other ingredients to the meat mixture such as defrosted peas, sweetcorn or chopped mixed peppers. Just add them before you put the mixture in the ovenproof dish.

grating the carrot

5 At this point, check the potatoes and if they are cooked, drain using a colander. Return the potatoes to the saucepan away from the heat. Add the butter, milk and a pinch of salt and pepper and mash until there are no lumps.

6 Spoon the mashed potato over the meat mixture and smooth to the edges of the dish. You can use a spoon to make a lovely pattern. If using cheese, sprinkle this across the top. Place the dish in the oven and bake for 45 minutes until crisp and golden on top.

3 Add the garlic, onions, celery, carrot, leeks and thyme and cook for 2–3 minutes. Add the tomato purée cook for a further minute over a medium heat.

4 Turn down the heat to low. Add the Worcestershire sauce and crumble the stock cube into the pan. Stir well. Season with salt and pepper to taste. Empty the mixture into the oven proof dish and set aside to cool slightly.

spreading the potato

mashing the potato

making patterns

vegetable lasagne

A classic Italian dish for the whole family. It is really tasty and filling and makes a great alternative to a traditional Sunday lunch. Eat this with lots of crispy green salad.

SERVES **4–6** • PREPARATION TIME: **35 MINUTES** • COOKING TIME: **30-45 MINUTES**

SHOPPING LIST

- 2 tbsp olive oil
- 2 medium onions, peeled and chopped
- 2 garlic cloves, peeled and chopped or crushed
- 1 large aubergine (eggplant) cut into large dice
- 1 courgette (zucchini), sliced
- 2 peppers (any colour), diced
- Salt and pepper
- 3 tbsp chopped leek
- 2 tbsp chopped celery
- 1 tsp chopped fresh thyme
- 1 tsp dried mixed herbs
- 2 tsp tomato purée
- 2 x 400-g (14-oz) tins chopped tomatoes
- About 20 basil leaves
- 9 lasagne sheets
- 150 g (5 oz/1¼ cups) grated cheese

For the white sauce:
- 400 ml (14 fl oz/1¾ cups) milk
- 50 g (2 oz) butter
- 40 g (1½ oz/½ cup) plain (all-purpose) flour

you will also need

Sharp knife, large frying pan, chopping board, medium saucepan, small saucepan, measuring jug, measuring scales, ovenproof lasagne dish, wooden spoon, tablespoon, grater

Assemble all the ingredients and equipment you need. Make sure you understand what everything is, especially anything you haven't used before. Wash your hands and put on a clean apron.

1 Preheat the oven to 190°C (375°F/Gas mark 5). Heat the olive oil in a large frying pan over a high heat. Add the onion and garlic and cook for 1–2 minutes. Add the aubergine (eggplant), courgette (zucchini) and peppers and cook for 3–4 minutes stirring occasionally. Season with salt and pepper.

frying the onion and garlic

2 Add the leek, celery and herbs and cook for a further 1–2 minutes, stirring occasionally. Reduce the heat to medium. Add the tomato purée and cook for 2–3 minutes.

3 Stir in the chopped tomatoes and season with salt and pepper. Reduce the heat to low and cook for 3–4 minutes.

adding the chopped tomatoes

4 Meanwhile rip or shred the basil leaves. When the sauce has finished cooking stir these into the sauce and remove from the heat.

5 Now make the white sauce. Pour the milk into a clean medium-sized saucepan over a medium heat and bring to the boil, then remove from the heat. Put the butter and flour into a small saucepan over a low-medium heat and stir together until the butter melts to form a smooth paste (this is called a roux). Gradually add the warm milk, stirring continuously to stop any lumps from forming.

6 Once the milk has all been added bring the sauce to the boil for 1 minute. This removes the starch taste from the sauce. Remove from the heat.

7 Using a large spoon, put one third of the tomato sauce into the bottom of the lasagne dish. Lay three sheets of lasagne on top. Spread two tablespoons of white sauce over the lasagne sheets. Repeat this until you have used all the vegetable sauce and lasagne sheets. End with a layer of white sauce. Sprinkle the grated cheese over the top.

adding a layer of lasagne sheets

sprinkling cheese on the top

8 Bake the lasagne in the preheated oven for 30–45 minutes. Take care when removing from the oven as the dish will be very hot.

66 This is lovely and **filling** – and it's fun putting all the **layers** together! **99** **ALEX, 8**

homemade burgers

These burgers are tastier and healthier than the ones you can buy. You know exactly what is in them and you can perfect your own recipe. Serve with potato wedges and a crunchy salad.

SERVES **6** • PREPARATION TIME: **25 MINUTES** • COOKING TIME: **15 MINUTES**

SHOPPING LIST

• 1 large onion (approx 4 tbsp when chopped)

• 2 cloves garlic

• 500 g (18 oz) mince (lamb or beef)

• 1 egg, beaten

• 2 tbsp chopped fresh herbs (eg parsley, chives or tarragon)

• 2 tbsp breadcrumbs (see opposite)

• Salt and pepper

• Optional extras: ½ tsp horseradish or pesto, pinch of mustard powder or paprika

• Bread buns, lettuce leaves, sliced tomato and grated cheese, to serve

you will also need

Chopping board, measuring scales, sharp knife, mixing bowl, wooden spoon, cheese grater or food processor, frying pan or baking tray

Assemble all the ingredients and equipment you need. Make sure you understand what everything is, especially anything you haven't used before. Wash your hands and put on a clean apron.

1 If baking in the oven, preheat the oven to 200°C (400°F/Gas mark 6). Peel and finely chop the onion and garlic.

2 Put the mince, onion and garlic in a mixing bowl. Mix together well with your hands or a spoon.

whisking the eggs with a fork

66 I **love** these **burgers**! 99 **AMIRA, 11**

3 Add the beaten egg, herbs, breadcrumbs and a pinch of salt and pepper to the bowl and mix again well. If using any of the optional extras add these now and mix well.

using your hands to combine the mixture

4 Divide the mixture into six and shape into hamburgers.

shaping the mixture into burger shapes

5 The burgers can be cooked in three ways: **To fry:** heat 2 tbsp oil in a frying pan and cook on a medium heat for 5–6 minutes on each side or until cooked through. **To bake:** place burgers on a baking tray and cook in a preheated oven on 200°C (400°F/Gas mark 6) for 15 minutes or until cooked through. **To grill:** Cook under a preheated grill on a medium heat for 8 minutes on each side or until cooked through. Whichever way you choose, make sure the burgers are not red in the middle.

6 Serve in the bread buns with lettuce, a slice of tomato and some grated cheese. You can also serve with tomato ketchup and mayonnaise.

useful tip Potato wedges are really easy to make and are a healthy alternative to normal chips. Simply scrub potatoes and boil in their skins for 10 minutes. Cut into wedge shapes, place on a baking tray, drizzle with olive oil and bake in a hot oven (190°C/375°F/Gas mark 5) for 15 minutes or until crispy on the outside and soft in the middle.

chicken pie

A tasty dish which is perfect for a cold day. Using a pastry cutter cut out shapes from any leftover pastry to decorate your pie.

SERVES **2–4** • PREPARATION TIME: **35 MINUTES** • COOKING TIME: **20–25 MINUTES**

SHOPPING LIST

- 750 ml (1½ pints/3¾ cups) milk
- Salt and pepper
- 500 g (18 oz) boneless chicken (thighs, legs or fillets), cut into 2.5 cm (1 in) pieces
- 2 bay leaves
- ½ onion, peeled
- 4–5 cloves
- 75 g (3 oz) butter
- 60 g (2½ oz/½ cup) plain (all-purpose) flour
- 1 medium onion, finely chopped
- 1 clove garlic, chopped or crushed
- 1 stick celery, finely chopped
- 3 tbsp chopped leek
- About 400 g (14 oz) puff or shortcrust pastry
- 1 egg, beaten

you will also need

2 large saucepans, measuring jug, chopping board, sharp knife, slotted spoon, wooden spoon, colander, tablespoon, rolling pin, ovenproof casserole dish, fork, pastry brush

Assemble all the ingredients and equipment you need. Make sure you understand what everything is, especially anything you haven't used before. Wash your hands and put on a clean apron.

slicing the raw chicken

1 Preheat the oven to 200°C (400°F/Gas mark 6). Pour the milk into a large saucepan with a pinch of salt and pepper, the chicken and the bay leaves. Stick the cloves into the onion half (this is known as studding) add the studded onion to the pan.

2 Bring the milk up to the boil then reduce the heat so it gently simmers. Cook for 10–15 minutes then remove from the heat.

3 Using a slotted spoon, remove the chicken from the milk but keep the milk as you will use it to make the sauce. Throw away the onion and the bay leaves.

making a roux sauce

6 Reduce the heat and simmer for 2–3 minutes. Add the chicken and any other optional extras and stir. Put the pie filling into the casserole dish.

7 Dust a clean work surface with flour and roll out the pastry on to this. Using the rolling pin to lift the pastry, roll it over the top of the casserole dish. Allow some pastry to hang over the edge of the dish as this allows for any shrinkage.

8 Brush the pastry with the beaten egg. Use the fork to press the edges of the pastry to the rim of the dish.

removing the poached chicken from the pan

4 Melt the butter in a clean saucepan and gently fry the chopped onion, garlic, celery and leek. Add the flour and cook over a medium heat for 3–4 minutes to make a roux sauce.

5 Carefully add the milk that you saved, stirring continuously to ensure that no lumps form, until all the milk is added.

rolling the pastry over the casserole dish

" This pie is **good** because you can add **extra** things to the mixture! **"** **NAOMI, 7**

optional extras Add 4–5 tbsp of any of the following: sweetcorn, peas, diced peppers, pancetta, cooked bacon, sliced mushrooms.

9 Place the pie onto the middle shelf of the preheated oven and bake for 20–25 minutes or until the pie is crisp, golden brown and cooked through.

risotto with peas and mint

The combination of peas and mint gives this classic dish fresh and exciting flavours. Yummy!

SERVES **2–4** • PREPARATION TIME: **20 MINUTES** • COOKING TIME: **20 MINUTES**

SHOPPING LIST

- 1.25 l (2½ pints/5¼ cups) boiling water
- 2 vegetable or chicken stock cubes
- 1 medium onion
- 2 garlic cloves
- 1 tbsp olive oil
- 50 g (2 oz) butter
- 300 g (10 oz/1½ cups) risotto rice
- 150 g (5 oz/1 cup) peas (fresh or defrosted from frozen)
- 50 g (2 oz/¼ cup) grated Parmesan cheese
- 10–12 fresh mint leaves, chopped
- Salt and pepper

you will also need

Measuring jug, wooden spoon, chopping board, sharp knife, cheese grater, large saucepan, ladle

Assemble all the ingredients and equipment you need. Make sure you understand what everything is, especially anything you haven't used before. Wash your hands and put on a clean apron.

1 Pour the boiling water into a measuring jug and crumble in the stock cubes. Stir to dissolve the cube and set aside.

2 Peel the onion and garlic and chop finely.

crumbling the stock cubes into the water

adding the rice to the pan

3 Heat the olive oil and 25 g (1 oz) of butter in a large saucepan over a medium heat until the butter has melted and is combined with the oil.

4 Add the onion and garlic and cook until soft, this will probably take about 2 minutes. Add the rice and cook for a further 1–2 minutes and stir, making sure each grain of rice is coated.

5 Add a ladleful of the stock you made earlier and stir well. When the stock has evaporated add another ladleful of stock and repeat until most of the stock is in the pan with the rice.

6 Continue to cook for 10–12 minutes, adding a ladleful of stock whenever the stock has been absorbed. Check the rice – it should have a fluffy, creamy texture with a little 'bite' to it. Make and add more stock if necessary.

7 Add the peas, grated cheese, mint leaves, remaining butter, a small ladleful of stock and leave for 2 minutes before stirring.

8 Season with a pinch of salt and pepper and serve hot.

teatime treats and party food

Here are some simple teatime meals to enjoy after a busy day at school or active weekend. Why not invite a friend round and get cooking together? You'll also find recipes for tasty treats here so you can impress your guests with your homemade creations!

spaghetti bolognaise

This is a famous Italian dish. The rich flavour and colour comes from the tomatoes, which are full of goodness. In fact tomatoes are often referred to as a superfood!

SERVES **4–6** • PREPARATION TIME: **30 MINUTES** • COOKING TIME: **25 MINUTES**

SHOPPING LIST

- 1 tbsp olive oil
- 500 g (18 oz) mince (beef or lamb)
- 1 large onion, peeled and chopped
- 1 stick celery, chopped
- 3 cloves garlic, chopped or crushed
- 1 small carrot, peeled and chopped
- 3 tbsp chopped leek
- 1 tsp dried mixed herbs or oregano
- 1 tsp fresh chopped thyme
- 1 stock cube (chicken or vegetable)
- 2 tsp tomato purée
- 2 x 400-g (14-oz) tins chopped tomatoes
- Salt and pepper
- 300 g (11 oz/2½ cups) spaghetti (or other pasta shapes)
- Grated Parmesan or Cheddar cheese (optional), to serve

you will also need

2 large saucepans, measuring scales, wooden spoon, chopping board, sharp knife, vegetable peeler, colander, cheese grater

Assemble all the ingredients and equipment you need. Make sure you understand what everything is, especially anything you haven't used before. Wash your hands and put on a clean apron.

cooking the spaghetti

1 Heat 1 tbsp olive oil in a large saucepan over a medium heat. Add the mince to the pan and cook for 3-4 minutes or until browned stirring occasionally and breaking down the mince with a wooden spoon.

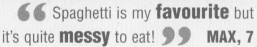
66 Spaghetti is my **favourite** but it's quite **messy** to eat! **99**   **MAX, 7**

spooning the bolognaise over the spaghetti

2 Add the chopped onion, celery, garlic, carrot and leek to the pan along with the dried herbs and thyme. Crumble the stock cube into the pan and stir well. Cook for a further 2–3 minutes.

3 Add the tomato purée and cook for 1 minute. Add the tins of chopped tomatoes and stir. Season with a pinch of salt and pepper. Reduce the heat and cook for a further 15–20 minutes.

4 Meanwhile, fill a large deep saucepan three-quarters full with water and add 1 tsp salt and 1 tsp olive oil and bring to the boil.

5 Very carefully place the spaghetti into the pan. The spaghetti will begin to bend with the heat of the water so it will all be covered by the water. Cook for about 10–12 minutes (check the instructions on the packet). The spaghetti should be soft but still have some 'bite'. When the spaghetti is cooked, drain using a colander.

6 Serve the spaghetti topped with some of the bolognaise sauce. Sprinkle on some grated cheese, if using.

tuna and sweetcorn fajitas

Fajitas are a popular meal from Mexico where the pancake-like tortillas are made with different grains. Eat them cold or warm with different fillings.

SERVES **4** • PREPARATION TIME: **20 MINUTES**

SHOPPING LIST

• 2–3 crisp lettuce leaves, such as iceberg

• 2 spring onions (scallions)

• 200 g (7 oz/1 cup) tinned tuna, drained

• 3 tbsp sweetcorn

• 5–6 tbsp mayonnaise

• Sliced cucumber and tomato (optional)

• Salt and pepper

• Pinch of paprika

• 8 flour tortillas

OPTIONAL EXTRAS

Add 1–2 tbsp of the following to your mixture: chopped mixed peppers, capers, chopped fresh herbs such as parsley or chives

you will also need

Chopping board, sharp knife, colander, tin opener, mixing bowl, fork, tablespoon

Assemble all the ingredients and equipment you need. Make sure you understand what everything is, especially anything you haven't used before. Wash your hands and put on a clean apron.

1 Wash the lettuce leaves and drain using the colander. Carefully chop the spring onions (scallions) and shred the lettuce leaves.

2 Put the tinned tuna in a mixing bowl with the mayonnaise and mix together well using the fork. Add the sweetcorn and chopped spring onions (scallions) and mix well. Season with a pinch of salt, pepper and paprika and mix again.

spreading the tuna mix onto the tortilla

3 Take one flour tortilla and spread one tablespoon of your tuna mixture into the centre of it. If you want to add any of the optional extras do this now and mix them in.

4 Sprinkle some shredded lettuce on to the filling and if you are adding any tomatoes or cucumber, lay these on top of the lettuce.

5 Fold up the bottom edge of the tortilla and then fold in both sides of the tortilla so you have a tortilla pocket. Repeat this process until you have used up all the filling.

folding up the tortilla

chop suey

A Chinese-inspired dish. Stir-frying the vegetables is a really quick way of cooking them without losing any crunch or vitamins.

SERVES **4** • PREPARATION TIME: **15–20 MINUTES** • COOKING TIME: **10 MINUTES**

SHOPPING LIST

- 750 ml (1½ pints/3¼ cups) boiling water
- 75 g (3 oz/¾ cup) noodles
- 2 tbsp oil
- 1 garlic clove, peeled and chopped
- 1 cm (½ in) piece ginger, peeled and chopped
- 1 stick celery, chopped
- 1 onion, peeled and chopped
- 1 carrot, peeled and chopped
- 50 g (2 oz) beansprouts
- 150 g (5 oz) peppers, chopped (any colour)
- 75 g (3 oz) broccoli florets
- 25 g (1 oz) mange tout
- 75 ml (3 fl oz/⅓ cup) water
- 2 tbsp soy sauce
- 1 vegetable stock cube
- 1 tsp cornflour (cornstarch)
- 3 tsp water
- 3 tbsp chopped fresh coriander (cilantro)

you will also need

Measuring jug, measuring scales, heatproof mixing bowl, colander, sharp knife, chopping board, wok or very large saucepan, vegetable peeler, wooden spoon, small mixing bowl, teaspoon

Assemble all the ingredients and equipment you need. Make sure you understand what everything is, especially anything you haven't used before. Wash your hands and put on a clean apron.

1 Pour the boiling water into the heatproof mixing bowl or jug. Carefully place the noodles into the boiling water and allow to soak for 5 minutes, stirring occasionally to separate the noodles.

soaking the noodles in boiling water

66 Stir-fries are so **easy** – I make them all the time now! 99 **OLIVIA, 12**

2 Drain the noodles using the colander. Allow to cool and then roughly chop the noodles and return to the bowl or jug.

3 Heat 1 tablespoon of oil in a wok or a very large pan over a medium/high heat.

4 Add the garlic and the ginger and all the vegetables and cook for 3–4 minutes stirring occasionally.

5 Reduce the heat and add 75 ml (3 fl oz/⅓ cup) water and the soy sauce.

6 Crumble the stock cube into the pan and stir. Add the noodles to the pan and stir well.

adding cornflour and water to the stir-fry

7 In a mixing bowl dissolve 1 teaspoon of cornflour (cornstarch) into 3 teaspoons of water. Add this to the pan and bring to the boil.

8 Remove from the heat, add the coriander (cilantro), mix well and serve.

nice and spicy rice

This is a yummy way to get lots of energy, vitamins and minerals. All the wonderful flavours come from herbs and spices so you do not need any salt.

SERVES **4** • PREPARATION TIME: **20 MINUTES** • COOKING TIME: **20 MINUTES**

SHOPPING LIST

- 200 g (7 oz/1 cup) basmati rice
- 1 tbsp oil
- 1 large onion, peeled and chopped
- 2 cloves garlic, peeled and sliced
- 1 cm (½ in) piece of ginger, peeled and chopped
- 2 whole cloves
- 1 stick cinnamon
- 2 cardamom pods, cracked
- 1½ tsp medium curry powder
- 50 g (2 oz/⅓ cup) frozen peas, defrosted
- 50 g (2 oz) sweetcorn
- 50 g (2 oz) peppers, chopped
- 1 stock cube dissolved in 375 ml (12 fl oz/1½ cups) boiling water
- 50 g (2 oz) flaked almonds (optional)

you will also need

Mixing bowl, large saucepan, wooden spoon, sharp knife, colander or sieve, dessert spoon, measuring jug, teaspoon, measuring scales, oven gloves, ovenproof dish

Assemble all the ingredients and equipment you need. Make sure you understand what everything is, especially anything you haven't used before. Wash your hands and put on a clean apron.

1 Preheat the oven to 180°C (360°F/Gas mark 4). Rinse and soak the rice in the mixing bowl for 10 minutes.

2 While the rice is soaking, heat the oil in a large saucepan. When the oil is hot, add the onions, garlic and ginger. Cook on a low heat until the onions are soft and have lost their colour.

3 Add the cloves, cinnamon and cardamom pods and cook for a further 2 minutes on a low heat. Add the curry powder and cook for a further 2 minutes, stirring continuously.

"I love **sticky** rice – you can add your **favourite** things to it!" **AMY, 12**

4 Drain the rice and add it to the saucepan. Stir so that the rice is coated in the oil and spices. Add the peas, sweetcorn, peppers and any other vegetables. Pour in the stock and stir.

5 Transfer the rice to an ovenproof dish and sprinkle with the flaked almonds. Cover with foil and place in the preheated oven and cook for 15–20 minutes. Remove from the oven and serve.

adding the rice to the pan

covering the rice with foil

chicken or fish bites

These delicious chicken or fish bites can be shallow-fried or baked in the oven but remember that baking in the oven is the healthier option.

SERVES **4** • PREPARATION TIME: **15 MINUTES** • COOKING TIME: **10-12 MINUTES**

SHOPPING LIST

- 450–500 g (16–18 oz) chicken or fish fillet (e.g. cod, plaice)
- 25–30 g (1–1½ oz/¼ cup) plain (all-purpose) flour
- 1–2 eggs
- 75 g (3 oz/¾ cup) breadcrumbs (see tip, page 65)
- Salt and pepper
- Zest of 1 lemon
- 2 tbsp chopped parsley (or other fresh herb)
- 3–4 tbsp olive oil (if frying)

cutting the fish into chunks

1 Carefully cut the chicken or fish into bite-sized pieces.

2 Put the flour into a mixing bowl. In a separate bowl, crack the eggs and whisk lightly and then season with a pinch of salt and pepper. Put the breadcrumbs, lemon zest and chopped herbs into another bowl.

3 Put a piece of chicken or fish into the flour bowl and coat. Then put it into the egg and coat. Finally roll the chicken or fish pieces in the breadcrumb mixture. Repeat this process until all the chicken or fish are covered in breadcrumbs.

you will also need

Sharp knife, chopping board, 3 mixing bowls, whisk or fork, baking tray or frying pan

Assemble all the ingredients and equipment you need. Make sure you understand what everything is, especially anything you haven't used before. Wash your hands and put on a clean apron.

dipping the pieces in flour, egg and breadcrumbs

66 These chicken **nuggets** are lovely and **crispy**! 99

ARWA, 10

4 If baking, preheat the oven to 200°C (400°F/ Gas mark 6). Place the chicken or fish pieces onto a baking tray and bake for 10–12 minutes until golden brown or until the chicken or fish is cooked through. The length of time will vary depending on the size of the chicken or fish pieces.

5 If frying, heat 1 teaspoon of oil in a frying pan over a medium heat. Place the chicken or fish in the pan and cook for 2–3 minutes turning the pieces half way through. You may need to add a little more oil to the pan after turning the pieces to make sure the breadcrumbs don't burn. You might need to fry the pieces in more than one batch depending on the size of your frying pan.

note When chicken and fish is cooked through, it will be white in colour in the middle. If there are any pink traces visible, this means it is not fully cooked and should be returned to the oven or pan and cooked for longer.

good idea Why not make a dip for these delicious bites? Sour cream is great mixed with some chopped chives or you could mix a little crushed garlic and some lemon juice with some mayonnaise.

mini quiches

These individual quiches are much more fun to serve than a large one. They make a delicious dish at teatime and you can also make them in advance and serve them for a party.

SERVES **4** • PREPARATION TIME: **40 MINUTES** • COOKING TIME: **20–25 MINUTES** • COOLING TIME: **5–10 MINUTES**

SHOPPING LIST

- 225 g (8 oz/2¼ cups) plain (all-purpose) flour
- 100 g (4 oz) butter
- 2–3 tbsp cold water
- salt and pepper
- 3 medium eggs
- 125 ml (4½ fl oz/½ cup) milk
- 100 ml (4 fl oz/½ cup) single (light) or double (heavy) cream
- 8 cherry or baby plum tomatoes, halved
- 1 heaped tbsp chopped chives or chopped spring onions (scallions)
- 75 g (3 oz/¾ cup) grated cheese

you will also need

Measuring scales, whisk, measuring jug, rolling pin, 4 quiche tins (about 10 cm/4 in in diameter), fork, baking parchment or foil, baking beans, round-ended knife, sieve

Assemble all the ingredients and equipment you need. Make sure you understand what everything is, especially anything you haven't used before. Wash your hands and put on a clean apron.

rubbing the flour and butter together

1 Sift the flour and a pinch of salt into a mixing bowl. Add the butter and gently rub together with your fingers until the mixture looks like breadcrumbs.

2 Add the water until your mixture sticks together without being too wet. Cover the bowl with cling film and allow to cool in the fridge for 20 minutes. Preheat the oven to 170°C (340°F/Gas mark 3).

rolling out the pastry

pricking the pastry bases

3 Remove the pastry from the fridge and divide into 4 pieces. Roll the pastry out on a lightly floured surface and line the quiche tins with the pastry. Leave a little extra pastry overhanging the edge of the tin – this allows for any shrinkage during cooking. Prick the base and edges of the pastry with a fork to allow the pastry to crisp during cooking.

4 Lay a piece of baking parchment or foil over each tin. Weigh the parchment down with baking beans or rice. This stops the pastry base rising during cooking and is called 'blind baking'. Place in the oven and bake for 15 minutes.

5 While the cases are cooking, prepare the filling. Crack the eggs into a mixing bowl. Add the milk, cream and a pinch of salt and pepper and beat well. Pour this mixture into a measuring jug.

6 Remove the cases from the oven and remove the parchment and baking beans. Make sure you wear oven gloves and ask an adult to help you. Return the pastry cases to the oven and bake them for a further 5 minutes without the parchment and baking beans.

7 Remove the cases from the oven and divide the cheese, chives/onions, and tomatoes between the 4 pastry cases. Pour the egg mix on top of the fillings until the cases are three-quarters full. Return the cases to the oven and bake for 20–25 minutes until cooked and golden.

8 Remove from the oven and allow to cool for 5–10 minutes. Trim off any over hanging pastry with a round ended knife. Serve the quiches with a crisp green salad.

scrumptious barbecue chicken

Leaving raw chicken pieces in the sauce, or marinating, means that the chicken absorbs lots of flavour before you cook it. Make these in advance for a party.

SERVES **2–4** • PREPARATION TIME: **10 MINUTES** • MARINATING TIME: **30 MINUTES** • COOKING TIME: **40 MINUTES**

SHOPPING LIST

- 800 g (1¾ lb) chicken thighs or drumsticks
- 2 cloves garlic, crushed or chopped
- 2 tbsp sugar
- ½ tbsp light soy sauce
- 1 tbsp clear honey
- 2 tbsp tomato ketchup
- ½ tsp tomato purée (paste)
- 1 tbsp brown sauce or Worcestershire sauce
- Salt and pepper

you will also need

Mixing bowl, pastry brush, sharp knife, tablespoon, greased baking tray, wooden spoon, measuring scales

Assemble all the ingredients and equipment you need. Make sure you understand what everything is, especially anything you haven't used before. Wash your hands and put on a clean apron.

1 Mix together all the ingredients, apart from the chicken, in the mixing bowl to make the marinade.

2 Score the chicken pieces with the sharp knife. This means cutting through the skin of the chicken in diagonal lines.

scoring the chicken
pieces with a knife

placing the chicken on a baking tray

" I love **barbecues** because everyone joins in! **"** **MAX, 8**

3 Put the chicken pieces into the bowl of marinade and mix until all the chicken is coated. Cover with clingfilm (plastic wrap) chill in the fridge until required. You should leave the chicken in the fridge for at least 30 minutes before cooking so the chicken soaks up all the flavours of the marinade.

4 When you are ready to cook the chicken, preheat the oven to 200°C (400°F/Gas mark 6).

5 Put the chicken onto a greased baking tray and bake in the oven for 40 minutes or until cooked through and golden brown. You can check if the chicken is cooked through by using a skewer or a sharp knife to check the meat is not pink in the middle. When chicken is fully cooked it is white in colour.

handy hint When you barbecue always make sure your chicken is cooked really well. The meat must be white and have no pink in it at all. Other meats like sausages and pork must also be cooked properly to prevent food poisoning.

fishcakes

Make fish fun! These are easy to make and yummy to eat at tea time. You can make them with cod, salmon or haddock depending on what fish you can find or prefer.

SERVES **4** • PREPARATION TIME: **35 MINUTES** • COOKING TIME: **20 MINUTES**

SHOPPING LIST

- 500 g (18 oz) peeled potatoes
- 500 g (18 oz) fish (cod, salmon or haddock)
- 2 spring onions (scallions), finely sliced
- 2 tbsp chopped parsley
- 1 tbsp breadcrumbs (see tip, page 65)
- 1 egg, beaten
- Salt and pepper
- Flour for dusting
- 2 tbsp olive oil

you will also need

chopping board, sharp knife, large saucepan, colander, potato masher, large mixing bowl, medium saucepan, fish slice, plate, wooden spoon, frying pan, baking tray

Assemble all the ingredients and equipment you need. Make sure you understand what everything is, especially anything you haven't used before. Wash your hands and put on a clean apron.

1 Preheat the oven to 190°C (375°F/Gas mark 5). Carefully cut the potatoes into even-sized pieces and put them into a large saucepan. Cover the potatoes with cold water and boil for 15–20 minutes or until cooked.

2 Drain the potatoes and leave them in the colander for 5 minutes to remove any excess water.

3 Return the potatoes to the saucepan and mash until smooth. Put the mashed potato in a large mixing bowl and set aside.

4 Put the fish in a pan and half-fill with water. Poach or simmer for 10 minutes until cooked. Remove the fish from the pan using the fish slice and put onto a plate to cool.

These are easier than they look – and **shaping** the cakes is **fun**! JAKE, 10

poaching the fish

5 Flake the fish and add to the mashed potato. Add the spring onion (scallion), parsley, breadcrumbs, egg and a pinch of salt and pepper. Mix well with a spoon or you can use your hands.

combining the fish
mixture with your hands

handy hint Salmon, mackerel, trout and sardines are oily fish and rich in Omega 3. This keeps the heart healthy.

6 Divide the mixture evenly into eight and shape into fishcakes. Lightly dust each fish cake with a small amount of flour.

shaping the mixture into 'patties'

dusting the fishcakes
with flour

7 Heat the olive oil in a frying pan and fry the fishcakes until golden brown on both sides.

8 Place the fishcakes on a baking tray and bake in the preheated oven for 12–15 minutes or until cooked and hot in the middle. Serve with crispy green salad.

apple muffins

Apple and cinnamon is a classic combination. These are fun and simple to make and so yummy that all your friends will want one!

MAKES **8 MUFFINS** • PREPARATION TIME: **20 MINUTES** • COOKING TIME: **20–25 MINUTES**

SHOPPING LIST

- 2 eggs
- 100 g (4 oz) butter or margarine
- 100 g (4 oz/½ cup) caster (superfine) sugar
- 100 g (4 oz/1 cup) self-raising flour
- 1 tsp baking powder
- 50 g (2 oz) golden syrup
- 1 large cooking apple (about 300 g/11 oz)
- Large pinch of ground cinnamon

you will also need

Muffin cases, muffin tin, small bowl, fork, large mixing bowl, wooden spoon, sieve, vegetable peeler, sharp knife, chopping board, dessert spoon, wire cooling rack

Assemble all the ingredients and equipment you need. Make sure you understand what everything is, especially anything you haven't used before. Wash your hands and put on a clean apron.

putting the muffin cases in the tin

1 Preheat the oven to 200°C (400°F/Gas mark 6). Put the muffin cases into the muffin tin and set aside. Crack the eggs into the small bowl and whisk well with the fork.

2 Mix the butter and the sugar together in the large mixing bowl until the mixture is smooth and combined.

mixing together the
butter and sugar

3 Add half of the whisked eggs to the butter and sugar mixture and mix well. Sift half of the flour into the mixture and mix well again. Add the baking powder and the remaining egg and sifted flour and mix until everything is combined. Add the golden syrup and mix in well.

coring the apple

4 Peel and chop the apple into quarters. Remove the core of the apple and grate or chop finely. Add the cinnamon and chopped apples to your mixture and mix well again.

5 Using a dessertspoon, fill each muffin case three-quarters full with your apple cake mixture. Put them into the preheated oven for 20–25 minutes. Remove from the oven and allow to cool on a wire rack.

spooning the mixture into the muffin cases

handy hint Use cooking apples, such as Bramleys, as eating apples can go soggy during the cooking process.

These are **great** for popping in your school bag and sharing with **friends**! " CINDY, 11

chocolate brownies

Bake your own brownies and enjoy sharing them at teatime or at a party but don't give them all away! Serve with cream, ice cream or fresh fruit.

MAKES **12–16** • PREPARATION TIME: **20 MINUTES** • COOKING TIME: **25 MINUTES** • COOLING TIME: **30 MINUTES**

SHOPPING LIST

• 100 g (4 oz) butter

• 175 g (6 oz/1 cup) caster (superfine) sugar

• 75 g (3 oz/⅓ cup) muscovado brown sugar

• 125 g (4½ oz) chocolate (plain or milk)

• 1 tbsp golden syrup

• 2 eggs

• 1 tsp vanilla extract/essence

• 100 g (4 oz/1 cup) plain (all-purpose) flour

• 2 tbsp cocoa powder

• ½ tsp baking powder

you will also need

20-cm (8-in) cake tin, greased and lined, saucepan, measuring scales, wooden spoon, tablespoon, small mixing bowl, fork, teaspoon

Assemble all the ingredients and equipment you need. Make sure you understand what everything is, especially anything you haven't used before. Wash your hands and put on a clean apron.

place the butter, sugar, chocolate and golden syrup in a pan

1 Preheat the oven to 180°C (350°F/Gas mark 4). Put the butter, caster sugar, brown sugar, chocolate and golden syrup in a pan and melt gently on a low heat until smooth and lump-free. Remove the pan from the heat and allow to cool for 5–10 minutes.

2 Break the eggs into the small mixing bowl and whisk with the fork until light and frothy. Add the beaten eggs, vanilla extract, flour, baking powder and cocoa to the melted chocolate mixture and mix well.

3 Pour the mixture into the greased and lined cake tin and bake on the middle shelf of the oven for 20–25 minutes.

4 Remove from the oven and allow to cool for 20–30 minutes before cutting into squares.

cutting the brownies into squares

66 These **chocolate** brownies are like **heaven**! 99
ALASTAIR, 9

handy hint real chocolate must contain cocoa butter rather than vegetable oil or any other fats. Good chocolate usually contains 70% cocoa.

index

A
apple, to core 92
Apple muffins 91
avocado dip 32

B
balanced diet 10
Banana and mango smoothie 20
basting 54
bread rolls, Cheesy 28
breadcrumbs 65
brownies, Chocolate 94
burgers, Homemade 64

C
celery, to peel 31
Cereal mixed with fruit 16
Cheesy bread rolls 28
Chicken bites 82
Chicken pie 67
chicken, Roast 52
chicken, Scrumptious barbecue 86
Chocolate brownies 94
Chop suey 78
Creamy scrambled eggs 14

D
dips 83

E
eggs, Creamy scrambled 14
equipment 9

F
fajitas, Tuna and Sweetcorn 76
Fish bites 82
fish, to flake 56
Fishcakes 88
food groups 10, 49
Fresh fruit kebabs 40
Fruit cocktail 18

G
garlic, to crush 32

H
healthy eating 10
Homemade burgers 64
hygiene 8

J
juice 18

K
kebabs, Fresh fruit 40
Kedgeree 55

L
lasagne, Vegetable 61

M
Mini quiches 84
muffins, Apple 91

N
Nice and spicy rice 80

O
Omega 3 90
omelette, Spanish 47
onion, to chop 47
oven gloves 52

P
pancake fillings 25
Pancakes 23
parsley, to chop 46
pasta dishes:
   Spaghetti bolognaise 74
   Vegetable lasagne 61
   Warm pasta salad 44
pastry 84
pitta bread, to open 42
Pitta pockets 42
Potato and bean salad 37
potato wedges 66
preparation 8

Q
quiches, Mini 84

R
rice dishes:
   Kedgeree 55
   Nice and spicy rice 80
   Risotto with peas and mint 70
Risotto with peas and mint 70
Roast chicken 52
roux sauce 68

S
safety 8
salads:
   Potato and bean salad 37
   Warm pasta salad 44
Scrumptious barbecue chicken 86
Shepherd's pie 58
smoothie, Banana and mango 20
Spaghetti bolognaise 74
Spanish omelette 47
spring onions, to slice 38
Spring rolls 34

T
techniques 11
tin opener, to use 46
tools 9
Tuna and sweetcorn fajitas

V
Vegetable lasagne 61
Vegetable sticks with avocado dip 31
vegetable wedges, roast 54

W
Warm pasta salad 44

Y
yeast 29